W9-APF-766

25 Great Grammar Poems With Activities

By Bobbi Katz

Activities by Karen Kellaher

DISCARDED

SCHOLASTIC
PROFESSIONAL BOOKS

New York • Toronto • London • Auckland • Sydney • Mexico City • New Delhi • Hong Kong

For Barry and Wendy

Teachers may photocopy the poems and activities for classroom use. Bobbi Katz retains all other rights to the poems. No other part of this publication may be reproduced in whole or in part, or stored in a retrieval system, or transmitted in any form or by any means, electronic, mechanical, photocopying or otherwise, without written permission of the publisher. For information regarding permission, write to Scholastic, 555 Broadway, New York, NY 10012.

Cover design by Norma Ortiz

Cover illustrations by Rick Moran

Interior illustrations by Ellen Joy Sasaki

Interior design by Ellen Matlach Hassell
for Boultinghouse & Boultinghouse, Inc.

Poetry copyright © 1999 by Bobbi Katz.
Activities copyright © 1999 by Karen Kellaher. All rights reserved.

ISBN 0-590-98365-2

Printed in the U.S.A.

Contents

Introduction

From Poet to Teacher

Does the word *grammar* make you groan? Is teaching the difference between a noun and a verb as inviting as taking a spoonful of cod liver oil? The poems and activities in *25 Great Grammar Poems With Activities* will change all that. You and your students will start to see grammar as an exciting game! Throughout the book, I've used my best rhyme and rhythm to make the essential rules of grammar a lot of fun. Most of these poems were written from the points of view of verbs, nouns, and other grammar stars. These parts of speech actually "talk" to students, addressing them in a kid-friendly way. Together, the rhyme and personification in the poems will tickle young funny bones.

The Grammar Game

I have found that the game of grammar is a lot like my favorite sport—basketball. As with basketball, grammar becomes fun when we begin to play with skill. To help students gain valuable grammar skills, my "assistant coach," Karen Kellaher, and I have planned inventive activities and slam-dunk reproducibles to accompany the poems.

Why, students may ask, is grammar a game worth playing? After all, won't grammar-correcting devices on computers make knowing the rules irrelevant? That's a good question. Sometimes I ask myself if I'm just a grumpy old grammar grouch. I grit my teeth when someone says, "Him and me was . . ." Is it because I am hopelessly out of touch with what is important to know? I don't think so. My experiences in classrooms and beyond reinforce my belief that the ability—or lack of ability—to express oneself correctly in good English can open doors to opportunities or slam them shut. Good writing and communication skills give kids an advantage in almost every subject area. (How can teachers *not* respond positively to well-expressed ideas, even when we are supposedly evaluating only content?)

Helping ALL our students to speak and to write well helps level the playing field. Success is sweet! The better kids do in school, the more they will like it. And the better they will continue to do. There are other important reasons to teach grammar. For example, later on, knowing basic English grammar will help many students learn a foreign language. For other students, a well-written letter may be the key to a life-changing opportunity. And here's a very practical reason to include grammar in the curriculum: School districts across the country are giving standardized tests in grammar and composition as early as third grade. Have I convinced you that grammar is important?

Although good grammar is important, we all know that what feels familiar governs how we speak. And simply correcting students' grammar mistakes is not going to erase ingrained patterns. Instead, we must give kids the basic tools to restructure their language. So let's get going and learn some basic grammar moves!

How to Use This Book

- Encourage the students to keep their own collections of poems in a folder or binder. Pass out copies of the relevant poem before introducing a lesson.

- Use the first poem, "Rules Make the Game," as an exciting introduction to grammar. This poem was written as a motivating unit opener. See page 9.

- Use the poems to engage students. The poems will convey the essence of the most commonly used parts of speech and punctuation with humor and rhythm. Use the lesson plans and reproducible activities to reinforce key concepts from the poems.

- Poems are meant to be heard. You may start by reading the poem aloud to the class, but, if possible, have groups of two to four students present each poem to the rest of the class. The groups should practice reading the poem aloud to each other before presenting it. Students may read together in chorus, read alternate lines, or come up with their own plan.

- Read each poem aloud at least twice. After the first reading, introduce or review vocabulary. Each lesson plan includes a list of words you may want to target. For each vocabulary word, we have provided its part of speech and meaning.

- Note that examples of the featured element of grammar are set in heavy type to make them easier to identify.

- Plan to give a Grammar Exhibition Game at a school assembly or on the school playground. Kids can "play" different parts of speech and dramatize the poems. Encourage students to explore the poems' rhymes and to clap or bounce a ball to keep the poems' rhythms.

A Word from the Coach

Some people call me the Grammar Grouch.
Sloppy English makes me say,
"Ouch."
As your grammar coach,
I'm here to teach
the way to use
most parts of speech.
They're words
but they will talk to you
just the way that people do.
Often they'll make an explanation
using what's called personification.
Learning good English
is work that is fun.
And the scoreboard has room for everyone.
So hang in there.
Take every shot.
Give the Grammar Game the best you've got.

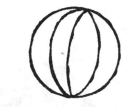

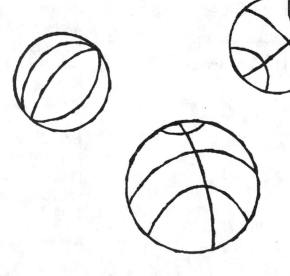

Rules Make the Game

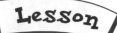

BACKGROUND

As the poem suggests, grammar is a set of rules for speaking or writing a language. Using correct grammar helps us communicate ideas clearly, just as following the rules of basketball helps us play a good game.

VOCABULARY

foul: ADJECTIVE against the rules

hubbub: NOUN confusion, uproar

pell-mell: ADVERB in a confused or disorderly way

TEACHING THE POEM

Discussion
What are some times we need rules? (*Possible answers: when we play sports, when we are working together in the classroom, when people live together in a community*) Why are these rules important?

Grammar Sleuths
Do we need to follow rules when we speak and write? To help students answer this question, play the Grammar Sleuths game:

1. Purposely make several grammar mistakes while addressing the class. For example, call a student "it" instead of "he" or "she," or write a student's name on the board in all lowercase letters.

2. As students laugh at or otherwise react to your errors, invite them to identify and correct the mistakes.

3. Point out that people have created language rules in order to make it easier to communicate.

K-W-L Chart
Invite students to brainstorm what they already know about grammar and what they would like to learn. At this point, it is not necessary for students to know and use correct terminology. For example, instead of stating that she wants to learn about proper nouns, a student may say that she wants to know when to use capital letters. Record students' ideas on a posterboard chart with three columns: What We <u>K</u>now; What We <u>W</u>ant to Know; and What We Have <u>L</u>earned. The third column will not be completed until after students have completed some lessons.

Practice
Ask students which two items this poem compares. (*basketball and grammar*) Then hand out the reproducible compare/contrast activity for students to complete (page 10).

Answers to Reproducible: Answers will vary.

Rules Make the Game

Could you have a good game of basketball
    if there weren't any rules—
        not *one* rule at all?
No particular court—just a stretch of bare floor.
No particular way to play or to score.
No moves that were foul. No moves that were fair.
Would you try your best? Would you even care?

Imagine you're starting to write one day,
    and there is *no* grammar!
        What could you say?
    There's a hubbub of words
        with no special spelling
            slip-sliding
                pell-mell—
    neither asking
            nor telling!
No questions. No statements. Not one exclamation.
        Ideas in a jumble.
        Piled-up punctuation.

Basketball and grammar—
    how are *they* the same?
Once you learn the rules, you can play either game.
Once you start to play, you'll start gaining skill.
The Grammar Team Players will help you.
        They will!
One by one they'll rap with you.
Have fun learning what they do.

comma   ver   oun

25 Great Grammar Poems   Scholastic Professional Books   © Bobbi Katz

Name _____

Rules Make the Game

How is grammar like basketball? Use
the poem "Rules Make the Game" and
your class discussion to write your answer.

_____

_____

_____

_____

What grammar rules can you think of? List as many as you can.

_____

_____

_____

_____

_____

_____

_____

_____

Nouns

BACKGROUND

Explain that nouns are words that name people, places, or things. There are several types of nouns. Common nouns name general people, places, or things (*doctor*, *store*, *car*), while proper nouns name specific people, places, or things (*Dr. Percy*, *Statue of Liberty*, *Mt. Everest*). Proper nouns always begin with a capital letter.

Another way to distinguish nouns is concrete versus abstract. Concrete nouns, like *pencil* or *soup*, are people, places, or things that one can see, hear, feel, or smell. Abstract nouns, like *peace*, *kindness*, or *anger*, name ideas or qualities that one cannot see, hear, feel, or smell.

You may want to point out that nouns can be singular or plural. This distinction is explored in another lesson plan (see page 44).

VOCABULARY

diva: NOUN a leading lady or main singer in an opera or concert

committee: NOUN a group of people chosen to discuss things and make decisions for a larger group

TEACHING THE POEM

Real-Life Grammar

Encourage students to label the nouns in your classroom (book, chalk, desk, closet, Cindy, Sam). Provide two different colors of sticky notes or construction paper; one for common nouns and one for proper nouns. Students can use masking tape to affix the labels to the appropriate people, places, and things.

Noun Storm

To help students identify nouns, play this game:

1. Write the letters of the alphabet on slips of paper and place the slips in a box or hat. Ask a student to randomly choose a letter from the hat.

2. Announce the letter to the class and explain that students will write as many nouns as they can think of that begin with that letter.

3. Allow students one minute to list their nouns. Use a watch with a second hand to measure the time.

4. When time is up, have students display their lists. Read aloud any unique or unusual nouns that begin with the designated letter.

Practice

Divide students into pairs and distribute one *Nouns* reproducible activity to each pair (see page 13). After students have completed the activity using the directions on the reproducible, they will have a humorous poem using plenty of nouns!

Answers to Reproducible: Answers will vary.

Nouns

A **noun** is
　　　a **person**,
　　　　　a **place**,
　　　　　　　or a **thing**.
Three **words** that cover a **lot**.

Once you start to think **people**
　　　　　and **places**
　　　　　　　and **things**,
it's hard to find **words** that are not!

Think **person**:
　　　brother, sister, teacher,
　　　tailor, sailor, doctor, preacher,
　　　taker, talker, walker, driver,
　　　drummer, dancer, diva, diver . . .
And *more* than one **person**?
Think **group, crowd, committee—**
　　　the **population** of a . . .
　　　　　place—
　　　　　a **city**.

Think **place**:
　　　park, meadow, cloud, court, pool,
　　　town, state, country, playground, school,
　　　office, market, street, trail, camp,
　　　highway, bridge, river, ramp . . .

Think **thing**:
　　　flower, flashlight, fire, flea,
　　　rhino, hippo, chimpanzee,
　　　color, crayon, water, fish,
　　　blanket, pillow, bed, dream,
　　　　　　　wish . . .

25 Great Grammar Poems　Scholastic Professional Books　© Bobbi Katz

Nouns

Now use your noun smarts to create a poem of your own. Ask a partner to provide the nouns for "A Noun Poem." Use the list below. When the list is complete, write the nouns in the poem. Do not let your partner see the poem until you are through!

NOUN LIST

1. Noun/Thing _____

2. Noun/Person (classmate) _____

3. Noun/Place _____

4. Noun/Place _____

5. Noun/Person _____

6. Noun/Person _____

7. Noun/Thing _____

A Noun Poem

My _____, my _____, I love it! It's cool.
       1   1

I'd like to buy one for _____ at school.
       2

I bring mine with me wherever I go,

from _____ to _____ to Colorado.
     3   4

My friends _____ and _____
        5   6

say a _____ is more useful.
     7

But I feel that I must remain truthful:

I will hold my _____ close to my heart.
       1

And hope that we never, ever must part!

25 Great Grammar Poems   Scholastic Professional Books

Proper Nouns

BACKGROUND

This poem is a wonderful follow-up to a general discussion of nouns. Remind students that common nouns name general people, places, or things, while proper nouns name specific people, places, or things. Proper nouns always begin with a capital letter. Frequently used proper nouns include the days of the week and the months of the year. Example: Monday was the 5th of July.

   Note: You may want to call attention to the word *Horrible,* which is capitalized in the poem. This is an example of a proper adjective. Because *Horrible* is part of Horrible Harold's name, the poet has used a capital letter. Other examples of proper adjectives include *American* flag, *White* House, *Impressionist* painting.

VOCABULARY

resides: VERB lives

specifically: ADVERB in particular

proper: ADJECTIVE formal; right or suitable for a given purpose

manor: NOUN mansion

TEACHING THE POEM

Discussion
Why do you think we capitalize the first letter of a proper noun? *(Possible answer: It is one way of alerting the reader that the noun is a specific or special person, place, or thing.)*

Noun Transformer
Write some common nouns on slips of paper and distribute the slips to students. Invite students to transform their common nouns into proper nouns by making the general word more specific. For example, a student might transform "street" into "Cherry Street."

All About Me
Have students create mini-books about themselves using as many proper nouns as possible. Students can write about their families, home towns, pets, favorite toys, favorite TV programs, beloved books, and most memorable vacations.

Practice
Distribute the *Proper Nouns* reproducible activity (page 16). Explain that each sentence contains one or more proper nouns that need to be capitalized. Ask students to circle the proper noun(s).

Answers to Reproducible: 1. Springfield, Massachusetts **2.** Mrs. Panzer **3.** Arrow Insurance Company **4.** Superman **5.** Westfield School **6.** White House **7.** Ralph **8.** Saturday **9.** *Charlotte's Web* **10.** Delaware River

Proper Nouns

Horrible Harold is not just a hamster.
He's **Miss Hattingham's** hamster.
That's **Horrible Harold**.
The place he resides is not just a house.
It's **Hattingham's Manor** of **Hillsbury Town**.
Hillsbury Town is right on a river,
not just any river.
No, that would not do!
Hillsbury Town is on **Billsbury River**,
which starts in the mountains and flows to the sea.
(The **Billsbury River**, specifically,
    goes from
        the **Mackintosh Mountains** to the **Finnegal Sea**.)

It would not be proper to be just a hamster,
    who lives with some lady
        in any old house
           in any old town
              on any old river.
It would not be proper, not proper at all!
It would not be proper at all!

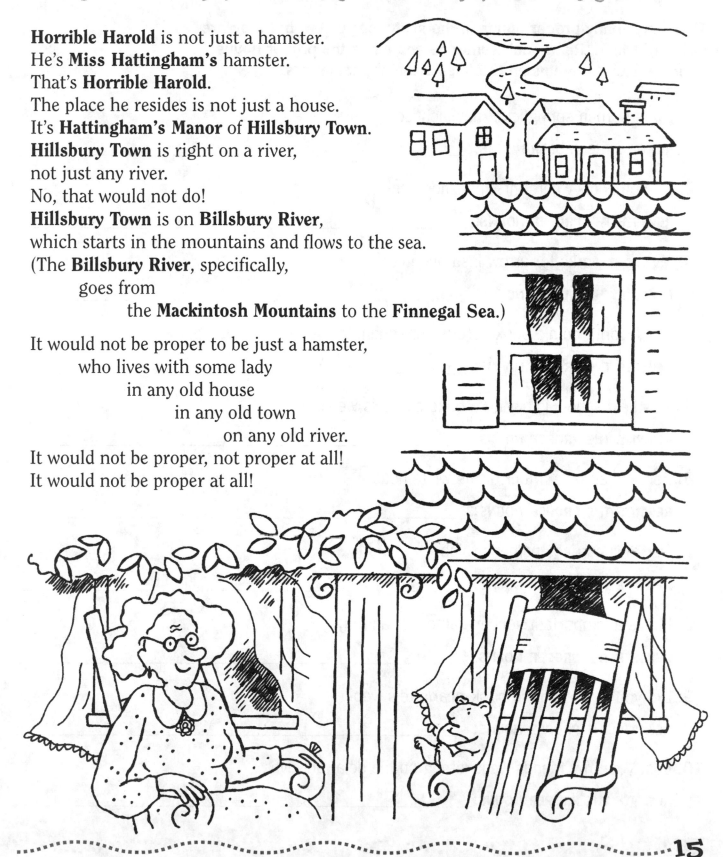

25 Great Grammar Poems Scholastic Professional Books © Bobbi Katz

Name _____

Proper Nouns

There are many proper nouns in the sentences below, but they are not capitalized. Read each sentence and circle the proper nouns. Then rewrite the nouns on the lines using capital letters.

1. I was born in springfield, massachusetts.

   REWRITE THE PROPER NOUNS: _____

2. Do you know where mrs. panzner went?

   REWRITE THE PROPER NOUNS: _____

3. My mom works for arrow insurance company.

   REWRITE THE PROPER NOUNS: _____

4. Her favorite comic book hero is superman.

   REWRITE THE PROPER NOUNS: _____

5. westfield school is having a bake sale this week.

   REWRITE THE PROPER NOUNS: _____

6. People can take a tour of the white house.

   REWRITE THE PROPER NOUNS: _____

7. Our mail carrier's name is ralph.

   REWRITE THE PROPER NOUNS: _____

8. I have an important soccer game on saturday.

   REWRITE THE PROPER NOUNS: _____

9. Did you ever read the book *charlotte's web*?

   REWRITE THE PROPER NOUNS: _____

10. Last year, my friends went rafting on the delaware river.

   REWRITE THE PROPER NOUNS: _____

25 Great Grammar Poems Scholastic Professional Books

Verbs Like Me

BACKGROUND

Explain that verbs are words that show action or a state of being. Some action verbs describe activities that a person can see or hear (*run, shout, jump, lift, drive*). Other action verbs describe activities that one cannot really see or hear (*think, learn, care*). Verbs that show a state of being are called linking verbs. They do not show action. Instead, they connect the subject of a sentence to another noun or adjective. Some examples of linking verbs are:

- Chelsea *is* intelligent.
- My brother *seems* tired.

You may also want to introduce the concept of verb tense at this point. Explain to students that verbs tell us if something happened in the past, is happening now, or will happen in the future.

VOCABULARY

claim: VERB to say that something is true

depend: VERB to rely on someone or something

TEACHING THE POEM

Verb Challenge

After presenting the poem, ask students to imagine that the verbs are speaking. Ask students to test the claim that nouns depend on verbs to show action. Can students write at least one sentence that does not have a verb? Afterward, review students' work and discuss the exercise. Point out that although one can write a sentence with no noun (*Go away!*), it is impossible to write a sentence with no verb.

Verb Charades

Have students take turns acting out verbs for the class to identify. Students might want to begin with some of the action verbs found in this poem (*see, walk, talk, climb*, and so on), then move on to more challenging verbs. Remind students that all answers must be in verb form.

Verb Sounds

Invite students to brainstorm verbs that actually sound like the actions they describe. Some fun examples are *crunch, sigh, creak, drip*, and *whistle*.

Practice

Distribute the *Verbs Like Me* reproducible activity to students (page 19). Encourage students to write short adventure stories using the verbs from the verb box.

Answers to Reproducible: Answers will vary.

Verbs Like Me

Nouns **claim to run** the grammar game
because of all the things they **name**.
Just **think** a minute.
    Look and **see**.
        Nouns **depend** on verbs like me.

A person **could** not **walk** or **talk**,
play ball, or **climb** a tree.

Any place that you **can name**
could not even **be**.

As far as things, **forget** it, kid!
Things just **don't stand** a chance.
Without a verb
    a bell **can't ring**,
        a bear **can't dance**,
        a bird **can't sing**.
The sun **can't shine**.
    The moon **can't glow**.
        Trees **need** verbs **to make** them **grow**.

Now you **know** why verbs **expect**
nouns **to give** us some respect.

25 Great Grammar Poems   Scholastic Professional Books   © Bobbi Katz

Verbs Like Me

Write a short action-adventure story on the lines below. Use at least five action verbs from the verb box, plus any other verbs that you think of on your own. If you need more space, use another sheet of paper.

Note: The verbs in the box are all in the past tense. If you'd like, you can change the verbs to make your story happen in the present or the future.

VERBS

tackled	wiggled	dropped
opened	laughed	glowed
slid	called	rattled
jumped	pulled	landed
peeked	twirled	sang

Adjectives in Short

BACKGROUND

Adjectives are words that modify, or describe, nouns or pronouns. Adjectives can tell how many (*ten* pencils) or what kind (a *long* book).

In addition to exploring adjectives, students may be interested in learning more about the poetry forms being featured. A *haiku* is a poem written in three lines. The first line is five syllables long, the second is seven syllables long, and the last is five syllables long. A *cinquain* is a five-line poem. The first line is a single word, usually a noun. The next three lines expand and explore that word: the second line does it with two words, the third line with three, and the fourth line with four. The fifth line either repeats the first word or is a synonym for it. A *quatrain* is a four-line stanza with a rhyme pattern. A *limerick* is a funny poem written in five lines with an AABBA rhyme scheme.

VOCABULARY

balmy: ADJECTIVE mild

frigid: ADJECTIVE extremely cold

nippy: ADJECTIVE chilly or cold

TEACHING THE POEM

Discussion

After reading the poems with students, ask them to describe the role adjectives play in the poems. Would the poems be as effective without adjectives? (*Possible answer: Adjectives help paint a mental picture of something.*)

The "Very" Ban

Encourage students to use a variety of rich adjectives instead of the word *very*. To help students get started, write some "very" phrases on the board and invite students to replace each phrase with a more specific and colorful adjective. Some examples:

- very big (enormous, huge, gigantic)
- very smart (brilliant, intelligent, bright)
- very bad (horrible, terrible, rotten)

Greeting Card

Have students create custom greeting cards for parents or friends by creating a simple acrostic poem with adjectives. Here's how:

1. Fold a piece of construction paper in half, so the opening is at the right.
2. Write the letters of the person's name down the left side of the paper.
3. For each letter, write an adjective that describes the person.
4. Write a message on the inside of the card and deliver it to a family member or friend. Here is an example:

> **M**arvelous
> **O**bservant
> **M**usical

Practice

Distribute the *Adjectives in Short* reproducible activity to students (page 22). Encourage each student to write his or her own haiku, using the syllable counts provided.

Answers to Reproducible: Answers will vary.

Adjectives in Short

HAIKU

adjectives flocking
telling about the noun "bird"
soft, feathery, blue

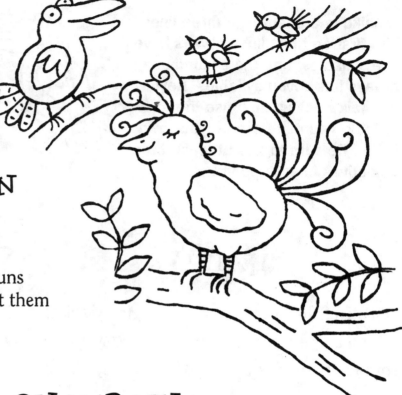

CINQUAIN

Adjectives
are words
coming before nouns
telling more about them
describing

QUATRAIN

**Sunny, calm, balmy, breezy,
chilly, frigid, nippy, cold** . . .
These adjectives describe the weather.
There are many more, I'm told.

TALL

LIMERICK

An adjective describing Paul
was painted upon a **blue** wall.
   The word wasn't **lazy**
   or **fresh** as a daisy.
The adjective painted was **tall.**

25 Great Grammar Poems   Scholastic Professional Books   © Bobbi Katz

Name _____

Adjectives in Short

A haiku is a poem with three lines. The first and last lines always have five syllables, and the second line always has seven syllables. Review the haiku below, then use the syllable counts to create your own haiku. Be sure to use at least three adjectives in your poem!

HAIKU

adjectives flocking   (5 syllables)
telling about the noun "bird"   (7 syllables)
soft, feathery, blue   (5 syllables)

YOUR HAIKU

_____   (5 syllables)

_____   (7 syllables)

_____   (5 syllables)

25 Great Grammar Poems   Scholastic Professional Books

Comparatively Speaking (Comparing Adjectives)

BACKGROUND

Explain to students that adjectives can be used to compare things. When we are talking about only one item, we use the positive degree of an adjective (*fast, nice, honest*). When we are comparing two things, we use the comparative degree of an adjective (*faster, nicer, more honest*). When we are comparing three or more things, we use the superlative degree of an adjective (*fastest, nicest, most honest*).

There are several ways to compare adjectives.

- For most one- or two-syllable adjectives, add -er and -est. EXAMPLE: *long, longer, longest.*
- For short adjectives that end in e, simply add -r and -st. EXAMPLE: *cute, cuter, cutest.*
- For short adjectives that end in y, drop the y and add -ier and -iest. EXAMPLE: *funny, funnier, funniest.*
- For most adjectives with two or more syllables, use the words *more* and *most*. EXAMPLE: *complicated, more complicated, most complicated.*
- Memorize the few adjectives that do not follow these rules. EXAMPLES: *good, better, best; bad, worse, worst.*

VOCABULARY

positive adjective: form of an adjective that describes one thing

comparative adjective: form of an adjective that compares two things, often ending in -er

superlative adjective: form of an adjective that compares three or more things, often ending in -est

TEACHING THE POEM

Discussion

After presenting the poem, call three of your tallest students to the front of the room. Have the class compare the three students' heights and make a statement using comparative adjectives. (*Possible answer: Jeff is tall; Grace is taller; Brian is tallest.*)

Adjective Olympics

To help students remember the degrees of adjectives, hold fun classroom contests. For example, students might vote on whose name is shortest, whose book bag is heaviest, and whose hair is longest. Award third, second, and first prizes for each category. Have students create a label for each winner that shows the appropriate adjective and degree. For example: Sarah: Longer Hair, Comparative Degree.

Comparative Cheer

Teach students this classic cheerleading chant to help them remember the unusual comparison for the adjective *good*: "Good, better, best! Never let it rest . . . 'til the good is better and the better is best!"

Practice

Distribute the reproducible activity for students to use to practice adjective comparisons (page 25).

Answers to Reproducible: 1. greener **2.** deepest **3.** hot **4.** most believable **5.** happier **6.** sweeter **7.** best **8.** nice **9.** earliest **10.** worse **11.** colder **12.** most tired **13.** prettier **14.** slow **15.** more talented

Comparatively Speaking

Positive, comparative, superlative,
WOW!
Adjectives and adverbs,
show us how
we can use you to compare
all sorts of things from everywhere.
If Jane runs **fast**
and June has passed her,
you would know that June runs **faster**.
But the **fastest** runner in the race
passed them both and takes first place!
Positive, comparative, superlative,
WOW!
Use all three to compare now:
Joe's jacket's **green**.
Jake's jacket is **greener**.
But the **greenest** jacket belongs
to Jim Beaner.

25 Great Grammar Poems   Scholastic Professional Books   © Bobbi Katz

Comparatively Speaking

Fill in the missing word or words in each of the adjective comparisons below. The first one is in the poem.

1. green, _____, greenest

2. deep, deeper, _____

3. _____, hotter, hottest

4. believable, more believable, _____

5. happy, _____, happiest

6. sweet, _____, sweetest

7. good, better, _____

8. _____, nicer, nicest

9. early, earlier, _____

10. bad, _____, worst

11. cold, _____, coldest

12. tired, more tired, _____

13. pretty, _____, prettiest

14. _____, slower, slowest

15. talented, _____, most talented

Adverbs

BACKGROUND

Adverbs can modify a verb, an adjective, or another adverb. When an adverb describes a verb, it tells when, where, how, or to what extent.

- She woke *early*. (when)
- He lives *nearby*. (where)
- Let's go *quickly*. (how)
- We enjoyed the show *thoroughly*. (to what extent)

When an adverb modifies an adjective, it often answers the questions "how?" or how much?" For example: It was a *really* cold day. When an adverb modifies another adverb, it also answers the questions "how?" or "how much?" For example: The children played *very* quietly.

Be sure to point out the final stanza of the poem, which explains that not all adverbs end in -*ly*. Some additional examples of adverbs that do not follow the -*ly* rule are *high*, *well*, *never*, *here*, and *now*.

VOCABULARY

specific: ADJECTIVE particular

lowly: ADJECTIVE humble

TEACHING THE POEM

Adverb-Packed News Report

News reports are full of adverbs; people want to know when, where, and how something happened. Some examples: *The suspect ran quickly; the fire spread swiftly; the governor spoke briefly.* After reading the poem with students, ask them to write brief news reports about events happening at your school or in your community. Their reports should include at least five adverbs.

Discussion

Invite students to discuss the parallels between adjectives and adverbs. Students probably understand the way an adjective modifies a noun. Point out that an adverb modifies a verb, adjective, or another adverb in much the same way.

Adverb List

Have kids go on an adverb safari by looking for adverbs in magazines, textbooks, and other reading material. (Note: Students can use this poem as a starting point.) Urge students to include unusual adverbs that do not end in -*ly*. List the adverbs on a large sheet of oak tag or chart paper and display the list so that students can see it from their seats. Students can use the list as a resource for writing.

Practice

Ask students to complete each sentence on the *Adverbs* reproducible activity with an appropriate adverb (page 28).

Answers to Reproducible: Answers will vary.

Adverbs

Verbs agree that we're terrific.
Adverbs make verbs more specific.
Adverbs appear **here** and **there**
    to tell you **when**,
        and **how**,
            and **where**.

Check us out.
    Can you guess why
        we tend to end with an l-y?
    That's an addition adverbs give
        to a lowly adjective.

A loud snore . . . Who's snoring **loudly**?
A proud man . . . Watch him march **proudly**!

Of course we don't all use l-y
to tell **how** much, **how** low, **how** high.

Words like **very**, **more**, **quite**, **so**—
are adverbs you should also know!

Adverbs

Read each sentence below. Then fill in the blank with an adverb that makes sense. Use your imagination!

1. She sang _____ to the crying baby.

2. Lionel read the book _____.

3. The computer printer works _____.

4. Last night, the whole family slept _____.

5. Peter is _____ busy.

6. We gathered _____ for the fire drill.

Now write some sentences of your own. Use the adverbs given.

7. Write a sentence using the adverb **politely**.

_____

8. Write a sentence using the adverb **really**.

_____

9. Write a sentence using the adverb **hardly**.

_____

10. Write a sentence using the adverb **nicely**.

_____

25 Great Grammar Poems Scholastic Professional Books

Pronouns

BACKGROUND

Pronouns replace nouns. There are several types of pronouns. The most common are personal pronouns.

- **Subjective personal pronouns** take the place of nouns that are the subjects of sentences.
  - **Singular:** *I you he/she/it*
  - **Plural:** *we you they*

- **Objective personal pronouns** replace nouns that are objects of a preposition or the direct or indirect object of the verb.
  - **Singular:** *me you him/her/it*
  - **Plural:** *us you them*

- **Possessive pronouns** show ownership.
  - **Singular:** *my your his/hers/its*
  - **Plural:** *our/ours your/yours their*

The poem introduces the word *antecedent*. The antecedent of a pronoun is the noun the pronoun is replacing.

- Margaret took the *dog* to the veterinarian because *it* had a broken leg. (antecedent = *dog*; pronoun = *it*)

- The *Wilsons* said *they* were heading to the park. (antecedent = *the Wilsons*; pronoun = *they*)

VOCABULARY

antecedent: NOUN in grammar, the word or phrase to which a pronoun refers

substitutes: NOUN things used in place of others; replacements

TEACHING THE POEM

Discussion

After reading the poem with students, ask them to imagine why people might have created pronouns. *(Possible answer: for ease of speaking)* Offer some humorous examples of what language might be like with no pronouns:

- Thea cooked the hamburger, then put the hamburger on a bun and ate the hamburger.

- Justin and Alyssa invited me to go to the movies with Justin and Alyssa.

Pronoun Bingo

This fun game reinforces important grammar skills. Here's how to play:

1. Distribute the *Pronouns* reproducible activity (page 31).

2. Ask students to fill the spaces in the grid with a variety of personal and possessive pronouns. They can choose from the following: *I, you, he, she, it, we, they, me, him, her, them, us, my, mine, your, yours, hers, his, their, theirs, its, our, ours, whose.*

3. Make up sentences in which a pronoun is missing. Read each sentence aloud and ask students to name the missing pronoun. For example:

   Tracy looked at the table and saw that _____ was dirty. (it)

4. Establish the correct answer, then instruct students to put an X through that pronoun if it appears on their grid. Students can cross out only one pronoun per turn, even if the correct pronoun appears on their card more than once.

5. Have students raise their hands when they find four pronouns in a row (vertical, horizontal, or diagonal). For a shorter version, stop the game when you are out of time and name the student with the most pronouns crossed out the winner.

Answers to Reproducible: Answers will vary.

Pronouns

Pronouns are ready to take the place
of any noun in the grammar race.
Although **we** may wear different suits,
all pronouns are noun substitutes.
Each pronoun promises,
"**I**'ll agree
with whichever noun
comes
ahead of **me**."
So please don't speak
as if a pronoun needn't
even have an
antecedent!
You'll see how good **your** game will be,
if **you** learn to use **us** properly.

25 Great Grammar Poems   Scholastic Professional Books   © Bobbi Katz

Pronouns

This is your Pronoun Bingo card. Write 16 pronouns in the boxes below. Your teacher will read aloud some sentences. Decide which pronoun is missing from each sentence, then look for that pronoun on your card. If you find it, put an X through the pronoun.

Articles

BACKGROUND

The words *a*, *an*, and *the* are called articles. These tiny words signal the presence of a noun. The article *the* refers to specific or known things (*the* car, not just any car). For this reason, it is called the **definite** article. The articles *a* and *an* are called **indefinite** because they refer to unspecified nouns. The indefinite article *a* is used before nouns beginning with consonants, while *an* is used before nouns starting with vowels (*a* plate, *an* orange).

VOCABULARY

forecast: VERB to say what you think will happen in the future; NOUN a report of what may happen in the future

convey: VERB to tell or to communicate

definite: ADJECTIVE specific or certain

indefinite: ADJECTIVE unspecified or uncertain

TEACHING THE POEM

Discussion

Begin by asking students to bring you various items from the classroom. Refer to the items using both definite and indefinite articles.

- Please bring me *a* book.
- Please bring me *the* book.

Chances are, when you use the indefinite articles *a* and *an*, students will be puzzled and ask you, "Which one?" Use this opportunity to introduce students to the words *a*, *an*, and *the*. Discuss the different functions each word has.

Discussion

After reading the poem with students, explore the difference between the two indefinite articles, *a* and *an*. As noted above, *a* precedes a noun that starts with a consonant. *An* precedes a noun that begins with a vowel. Write some correct and incorrect examples on the board and invite students to read them aloud. Students will find that the incorrect examples do not sound right. Encourage students to trust their ears when choosing an indefinite article.

- not *a umbrella*, but *an umbrella*
- not *an party*, but *a party*
- not *a apple*, but *an apple*
- not *an computer*, but *a computer*

Practice

Have students use the *Articles* reproducible activity to practice using the three articles correctly (page 34).

Answers to Reproducible: Answers will vary.

Articles

We forecast what a noun will be.
We're **a**, **an**, and **the**.
We're "The Articles Three."
We come before nouns
to convey
a hint of what a noun will say.
Is it something specific and *definite*?
The article "**the**" goes ahead of it.
In other words, if Michael shoots **the** ball,
it isn't just any old ball at all!
It's a specific ball,
most definitely,
and there's no question
which ball it might be.
Now suppose you want to buy **a** ball.
You might look at quite **a** few,
until you find **the** ball you want,
the ball that's right for you.
While you're looking, it's *indefinite*.
This ball? That ball? Which will you get?
But once you find **the** one for you,
it's *definite*.
No other ball will do.

25 Great Grammar Poems Scholastic Professional Books © Bobbi Katz

Name _____

Articles

After you have read the poem, practice using the articles *a*, *an*, and *the*.

The article *the* is used to show a specific noun.

EXAMPLE: Bring me *the* red ball, not just any ball.

Now write two sentences that use the article *the*.

_____

_____

The article *a* is used **before a noun that starts with a consonant.**

EXAMPLE: Bring me *a* pencil.

Now write two sentences that use the article *a*.

_____

_____

The article *an* is used before a noun that starts with a vowel.

EXAMPLE: Bring me *an* apple.

Now write two sentences that use the article *an*.

_____

_____

Write two sentences that use all three articles!

_____

_____

25 Great Grammar Poems Scholastic Professional Books

Prepositions Explain

BACKGROUND

Prepositions modify (tell more about) a verb, a noun, or pronoun. A preposition is followed by an object and forms a prepositional phrase. Here are some examples (prepositions are in italic, and prepositional phrases are underlined).

- The envelopes are *inside* the desk.

- I won't go out *without* an umbrella.

- *Despite* her cold, she won the race.

Some prepositions are two or three words: *in front of, according to, except for,* and *in back of.* For an extensive list of prepositions, see the poem and the accompanying reproducible activity.

VOCABULARY

position: NOUN the place where something is

object: NOUN The **object** of a preposition is the noun that follows the preposition.

modify: VERB to describe; to limit the meaning of a word or phrase

beautify: VERB to make something beautiful

TEACHING THE POEM

Discussion

Write some simple prepositional phrases on the board (*in the house, on the court, to the post office, outside the door, after the movie*). Circle the prepositions and ask students why these words are important. What do the words tell us? (*Possible answer: Prepositions often tell us where something is, where something is going, or when something happened.*)

Newspaper Hunt

To help students see the importance and prevalence of prepositions in the English language, encourage students to list all the prepositions they find in a newspaper or magazine article.

Practice

Distribute the reproducible activity (page 37) and ask students to use the prepositions to complete the sentences.

Answers to Reproducible: 1. on, by, at, around **2.** on, above, beneath, underneath, by, around **3.** in, inside, outside, after, of, at, about, before **4.** in, beneath, underneath, with, by, at **5.** by, about **6.** after, before **7.** to, after, with, without, by, at, around **8.** of **9.** outside, by, at **10.** in, inside

Prepositions Explain

If you were a preposition,
you'd be **in** a key position.
A preposition spends its days
heading a prepositional phrase.
The object **of** a preposition
takes the opposite position.
The object's always **at** the <u>end</u>:
beneath the <u>tree</u>,
around the <u>bend</u>.
Our phrases sometimes beautify,
but they will *always* modify.
When you see one, you'll know more
about a sentence than before.
When verbs and nouns are not enough,
that's when we will strut our stuff!
in…
        on…
            to…
                above…
                      beneath…
                          inside…   **outside**…
                          underneath...
before…   **after**…
       with…   **without**…
       by…
          of…
            at…
            around…
            about…

25 Great Grammar Poems   Scholastic Professional Books   © Bobbi Katz

Prepositions Explain

The prepositions from the poem are listed in the box below. Use a preposition from the box to complete each sentence. There may be more than one correct preposition for each sentence.

in	with	on	without	inside
by	above	of	beneath	outside
to	around	at	about	after
before			underneath	

1. My friend Liza lives _____ the corner.

2. Will you put the boxes _____ the table?

3. Let's talk _____ school tomorrow.

4. Pedro sat _____ the tree for an hour.

5. The winning essay was written _____ Julia.

6. We should go inside _____ it rains.

7. The dog ran _____ its owner.

8. He is one _____ my favorite sports stars.

9. Please leave your umbrella _____ the door.

10. I put the milk _____ the refrigerator.

Conjunctions

BACKGROUND

The most commonly used conjunctions are coordinating conjunctions, which join words, phrases, and sentences. These are *and, yet, but, nor, so,* and *or*. For example: *I wanted to see the movie but the tickets were sold out.* There are several other types of conjunctions. You may want to introduce these to older students.

- Subordinating conjunctions which join dependent to independent clauses. Examples: *after, as, because, than, when, while.*

- Correlative conjunctions which always appear in pairs. Examples: *either/or, neither/nor.*

- Adverbial conjunctions which join two sentences or clauses of equal importance. Examples: *however, nevertheless, so, therefore.*

VOCABULARY

link: VERB to join objects, ideas, or people together

functions: NOUN jobs or purposes

rarer: ADJECTIVE more unusual

TEACHING THE POEM

Discussion

The poem says, "Conjunctions always make connections." Ask students to discuss how words like *but* and *and* make connections. Have students offer examples of these or other conjunctions in action.

Hands-On Language Arts

For fun, have each student write a simple sentence on an index card. Encourage all students to focus on a single general topic, such as cafeteria foods or dogs. Then challenge each student to use a conjunction to link his or her sentence to someone else's. Students will enjoy roaming the room looking for a link that makes sense. You may want to list some common conjunctions on the board as a reminder to students. Examples of linked sentences:

- Our cafeteria's hot dogs are delicious, BUT the chicken patties are disgusting.

- Cats make fun pets, AND they are easy to take care of.

- Dogs are friendly, SO everyone should have a dog.

Practice

The *Conjunctions* reproducible activity (page 40) helps students become adept at using the common conjunctions *if, and,* and *but*.

Answers to Reproducible: 1. and **2.** if **3.** and **4.** but **5.** but **6.** and **7.** if **8.** and **9.** but **10.** if **11.** and **12.** but **13.** and **14.** If **15.** but

Conjunctions

Conjunctions always make
connections.
They link thoughts and give directions.
Two conjunctions,
but and **and**,
are conjunctions whose functions
are in great demand.

There are rarer conjunctions.
Please don't forget
nevertheless, therefore, thus, yet!

Conjunctions: Ifs, Ands, and Buts!

**Each sentence below is missing a conjunction.
Decide whether the missing conjunction is *if*, *and*,
or *but*. Then write the conjunction on the line.**

1. Hillary _____ Jaclyn both like science.

2. I will go to the beach _____ the weather is nice.

3. Stephan is class president _____ Isabel is vice president.

4. Jeannie is allergic to cats _____ she loves dogs.

5. My family's car is old _____ it still runs well.

6. I enjoy school _____ I hope to go to college one day.

7. You may borrow my sweater _____ you take good care of it.

8. Lily tossed _____ turned all night long.

9. Minnesota is cold _____ Alaska is even colder.

10. You should drink milk _____ you want healthy bones.

11. Kyle joined the school band _____ the basketball team.

12. I like to take pictures _____ I do not have my own camera.

13. Social studies _____ math are my favorite subjects.

14. _____ you lend me fifty cents, I can buy a soda pop for us to share.

15. The fire engine has its lights on _____ not its sirens.

25 Great Grammar Poems   Scholastic Professional Books

Upper Case and Lower Case

BACKGROUND

Experts believe that the first written letters were capitals. These letters were easy to carve into stone tablets or the faces of buildings. Later, when scribes wrote on expensive parchment, they tried to write quickly and fit many words onto each page. Capital letters were too large and difficult, so the scribes developed a system that combined capital letters with small letters. Incidentally, this system was in the cursive style.

Today we often call capital and small letters uppercase and lowercase. Uppercase letters are used at the beginning of a sentence, in acronyms and abbreviations (for example, U.S.), and in proper nouns. The pronoun *I* is also uppercase.

VOCABULARY

abbreviate: VERB to make something shorter

TEACHING THE POEM

Discussion

These two poems imagine that uppercase letters and lowercase letters have personalities. Which adjectives might describe each?

Alphabet Soup

List some well-known acronyms and abbreviations on the board and invite students to guess what they stand for. Some suggestions: U.N. (United Nations), NASA (National Aeronautics and Space Administration), RAM (random-access memory), N.B.A. (National Basketball Association). Then encourage students to create an acronym for your class or for a club to which they belong. For example: MACK (Mrs. Anthony's Cool Kids) or BEST (Brown Elementary Soccer Team). (Note: Point out to students that different newspaper, magazine, and book publishers sometimes have differing rules regarding when to use periods in acronyms and abbreviations.)

Noun Tic-Tac-Toe

Encourage students to play this simple game. Instead of using X's and O's, students will use proper and common nouns. The goal of the game is to get three proper nouns or three common nouns in a row. Students must remember to capitalize the proper nouns.

Memory Mobiles

To help students remember the rules for capitalization, have them create mobiles. Write the rules for capitalization on a large index card, then use string to hang cutout capital and lowercase letters from the card.

Practice

Students can use the *Upper Case and Lower Case* reproducible activity to determine which words ought to take a capital letter. (See page 43.)

Answers to Reproducible: 1. I **2.** Florida **3.** Dr. **4.** Oak **5.** Christa **6.** Let's **7.** Halloween **8.** Japanese **9.** Canada **10.** Girl **11.** Burger Barn **12.** The **13.** California **14.** Paul **15.** July

Upper Case and Lower Case

Poem

The Capital Letter: UPPER CASE

My friends call me UPPER CASE.
I'm a capital letter.
I'm in your face.
I'm bigger. I'm better.
I'm easy to see.
You can't start a sentence
if you don't use me.

What else do I do?
I'd better mention
        that I take positions
to draw your attention.
I send signals for you to sight
        when you read
and when you write.
Every proper noun you see
begins with a capital letter like me.
And, my, those nouns appreciate
the neat way I abbreviate.
Los Angeles becomes L.A.
Do you know the words for N.B.A.?

lower case letters

no one ever looks our way.
no one seems to care.
yet if letters had no lower case,
most words would not be there.

proper nouns need capitals.
that's how sentences begin.
but words appear in lower cases
on printed pages in most places.

25 Great Grammar Poems   Scholastic Professional Books   © Bobbi Katz

Upper Case and Lower Case

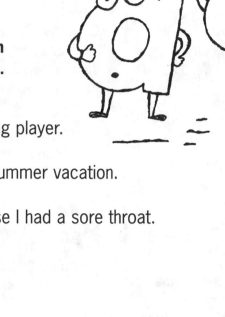

Read each sentence below. Then underline the word or words in each sentence that should be capitalized.

1. The coach said i was a promising player.

2. We are going to florida during summer vacation.

3. I went to see dr. Morgan because I had a sore throat.

4. Ronald lives on oak Lane.

5. My best friend is christa.

6. let's go to the park this weekend if it does not rain.

7. Ed's favorite holiday is halloween.

8. A japanese maple tree grows in my yard.

9. The United States shares a border with canada.

10. I would like to become a girl Scout someday.

11. They ate hamburgers and fries at burger barn.

12. the capital of Vermont is Montpelier.

13. Oregon is north of california.

14. paul was asked to go to the principal's office.

15. My birthday is at the beginning of july.

25 Great Grammar Poems   Scholastic Professional Books

Singular and Plural

BACKGROUND

This poem covers the basics of singular and plural nouns and verbs. There are several rules for making a singular noun plural.

- Add -s to the end of most singular nouns. (cat/cats)

- Add -es to singular nouns ending in ch, s, sh, x, or z. (bush/bushes)

- Drop the y and add -ies to a singular noun ending in a consonant followed by y. (penny/pennies)

- Add -es to words ending in o preceded by a consonant. (tomato/tomatoes)

There are exceptions to these rules. Some are: man/men, foot/feet, knife/knives.

   Explain that verbs will also be singular or plural, depending on the subject of the sentence. This is explored at greater length in the poem "Agreement" (page 51).

VOCABULARY

confess: VERB to admit something

exceptions: NOUN things that are not included in a general rule or statement

TEACHING THE POEM

Creative Writing

Have students create a rhyme or rhythmic rap to help them remember unusual plural nouns (children, men, women, feet, geese, deer, steer, and so on). For example:

Foot / feet / That's neat!
Man / men / Say it again!
Child / children / CLAP, CLAP, CLAP!
Let's put plurals in a rap.

Plural Game Show

Have students work in pairs to drill each other on plurals. One student should serve as the game show host, giving the contestant 20 to 25 singular nouns. The contestant must make the nouns plural, with the option of passing on any he or she does not know. After 60 seconds, the round is over and the contestant gets credit for all correct plurals. To add to the game show atmosphere, offer small prizes.

Practice

After reading the poem, distribute the Singular and Plural reproducible activity (page 46). Students will enjoy turning singular nouns into plurals, then hunting for the plurals in a word-search puzzle.

Answers to Reproducible:
1. gifts 2. mice 3. faces
4. people 5. pens 6. books
7. geese 8. men 9. parties
10. children 11. places
12. sashes 13. videos
14. bicycles

```
O C M G N S T I C N P
S H E B I G E E S E O
T U N O I F S P E N S
V B T C J O T W G U O
A S O M I C E R S M E F
S O K F E B H I E L V M
A K Z A F A R P J I P L
S H K H C K O C E D E A
H A U E V E N H D T O C
E D F S P Q S I T S E
S N B I C Y C L E S S
P T N E S U M D J Z
J I Y Z E L Y R U I B
E X P A R T I E S F T
M D S B K F H N A S E
```

Singular and Plural

There are certain basic rules
    you will need to know
      to get into the grammar game.
On your mark! Let's go!
    Singular means only one.
    Plural means two or more.
You have to know the difference,
or your sentences won't score.
Singular: one pan, one can, one shoe, one face, one space.
Plural: pans,

      cans,

          shoes,

             and faces,

                two

                  or maybe

                     many

                        spaces.

To make a noun plural add "s" or "es."
That's pretty easy, won't you confess?
    Exceptions
    give grammar and spelling
      more spice:
    one goose but two geese;
    one mouse but three mice.

Verbs are **singular** and **plural**, too.
Don't be tricked by what verbs do.
In the third person (he, she, it, or they)
when the verb is **plural**, the "s" slips away.
The **singular**: He thinks, She winks, It blinks.
The **plural** drops the "s": They think.
Why aren't rules for nouns and verbs the same?
Let's just chalk it up to the grammar game.

25 Great Grammar Poems Scholastic Professional Books © Bobbi Katz

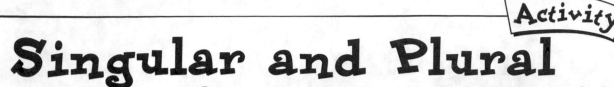

Singular and Plural

Activity

Turn each singular noun into a plural. Then find and circle the
plurals in the puzzle. Words can run across, down, or diagonally.

Singular   Plural

1. gift . . . . _____

2. mouse . . . . . . _____

3. face . . . . _____

4. person . . . . . . _____

5. pen . . . . _____

6. book . . . . _____

7. goose . . . . . . _____

8. man . . . . _____

9. party . . . . . . _____

10. child . . . . _____

11. place . . . . _____

12. sash . . . . . . _____

13. video . . . . . . _____

14. bicycle . . . . . _____

```
O C M G N S T I C N P
S H E B I G E E S E O
T U N O I F S P E N S
V B T C J Q T W G U O
A O M I C E R S M E F
S O F E B H I E L V M
A K Z A F A R P J I P
S S K H C K O C E D L
H A U E V E N H D E A
E D F S P Q S I T O C
S N B I C Y C L E S E
P T N E S U M D J Z S
J I Y Z E L Y R U I B
E X P A R T I E S F T
M D S B K F H N A S E
```

25 Great Grammar Poems   Scholastic Professional Books

The Truth About Sentences

BACKGROUND

This poem helps students remember that all sentences, long or short, have both a subject and a predicate. There are several ways to categorize subjects and predicates.

- A simple subject is the noun or pronoun that tells who or what the sentence is about. EXAMPLE: The *clerk* smiled.

- A complete subject is the noun plus any descriptive words that go with it. EXAMPLE: *The nice clerk at the grocery store* smiled.

- A compound subject is two or more nouns joined by a conjunction. EXAMPLE: *The clerk and the customer* both smiled.

- A simple predicate is the verb in a predicate. EXAMPLE: The girl *played*.

- A complete predicate is the verb plus any descriptive words that go with it to help explain the action of the sentence. EXAMPLE: The girl *played quietly with a stuffed animal*.

- A compound predicate is two or more verbs joined together. EXAMPLE: The girl *sat and played*.

Point out to students that a command usually has an inferred subject (as described in the last line of the poem). The subject in such sentences is "you," even though the subject is not stated.

- (You) Go to your room!
- (You) Wait for me!

VOCABULARY

merely: ADVERB only or simply

inferred: VERB concluded; guessed from the facts

TEACHING THE POEM

Hands-On Activity

Think of 10 to 15 famous sayings that are complete sentences (*An apple a day keeps the doctor away; A penny saved is a penny earned*). Divide each saying into its complete subject and complete predicate and write each on a separate index card. Distribute the index cards to students, then encourage them to compare their cards until they find their match. This activity also works well with movie and song titles.

Play E-S-P

This simple activity involves **E**stablishing the **S**ubject and **P**redicate of a sentence. Have students find a sentence in a book, magazine, or newspaper. Have them write the sentence on a line and draw a slash between the subject and predicate. This is the foundation of sentence diagramming.

Practice

After reading the poem, distribute the *Sentences* reproducible activity (page 49). Ask students to follow the instructions on the page to identify subjects and predicates, including the inferred "you."

Answers to Reproducible: 1. subject = boy, predicate = slipped **2.** subject = I, predicate = finished **3.** subject = He, predicate = remembered **4.** subject = store, predicate = opens **5.** subject = weather, predicate = forced **6.** subject = Dixons, predicate = live **7.** Go **8.** Look **9.** eat **10–12.** Answers will vary.

The Truth About Sentences

There hasn't been a sentence yet
without a subject or a predicate,
although at times,
as you may have heard,
the subject merely is inferred.

25 Great Grammar Poems   Scholastic Professional Books   © Bobbi Katz

The Truth About Sentences

As the poem states, all sentences have a subject and a predicate.
In each sentence below, circle the simple subject.
Underline the simple predicate.

1. The boy slipped on the banana peel.

2. I finished the book already!

3. He remembered the tickets.

4. The store opens at 7 o'clock.

5. The cold weather forced everyone to stay inside.

6. The Dixons live on the next block.

In each of the sentences below, the subject is "you."
Underline the predicate.

7. Go to the store.

8. Look at that roller coaster!

9. Please eat your vegetables.

Read each sentence below. On the line, write
a subject or predicate that makes sense.

10. _____ likes to play hide-and-seek.

11. Amber and Brittany _____.

12. The tall oak tree _____.

Agreement

BACKGROUND

This poem extends the concepts introduced in the preceding two poems, reminding students that the subject and predicate in a sentence must agree, or match. That means if the subject is singular (one thing or one person), the verb must also be singular. A plural subject, however, always takes a plural verb. Although this rule of thumb is easy to remember, it can be tricky to apply. For example, although an *s* frequently makes a noun/subject plural, an *s* usually signals a *singular* verb. In the present tense, a singular verb often ends in *s* (*it runs, she laughs, he sends*). A plural verb in the present tense usually does *not* end in *s* (*they run, we laugh, they send*).

VOCABULARY

subject: NOUN a word or group of words in a sentence that tells whom or what the sentence is about

predicate: NOUN the part of a sentence containing the verb that tells what the subject does or what is done to the subject

strategy: NOUN a clever plan for achieving a goal

TEACHING THE POEM

Discussion

After reading the poem aloud with students, invite them to answer the question at the end of the poem: "Mary have a little lamb. It's wrong! Can you figure out why?" Students should realize that the verb *have* is plural. It would be correct if the subject of the sentence were plural (for example, *Mary and Mark* or *They*). However, with the singular subject *Mary*, the verb should also be singular. The correct verb is *has* in the present tense or *had* in the past tense.

Verb Conjugation

To help students recognize the ways present-tense verbs change from the singular to the plural, introduce simple verb conjugation. You may want to write the pronouns *I, you, he, she, it, we,* and *they* on the board and invite students to come up and fill in the present tense of commonly used verbs. For example: *I run, you run, he runs, she runs, it runs, we run, they run.*

Practice

After reading the poem, distribute the *Agreement* reproducible activity (page 52). Students will enjoy checking for agreement in lines from famous Mother Goose rhymes.

Answers to Reproducible: 1. X **2.** A **3.** X **4.** X **5.** A **6.** X **7.** A **8.** X **9.** A **10.** A **11.** A **12.** X

Agreement

Winning sentences have one strategy:
All of the players need to agree.
A singular subject—it's a sure bet—
must have a singular predicate.
We say,
"Mary has a little lamb."
The subject, "Mary," is one.
The predicate, of course, is "has."
The sentence is well done.
We even could say, "Mary has ten sheep."
But, oh, how our coach would sigh
if we said,
"Mary have a little lamb."
It's wrong!
Can you figure out why?

Agreement

This poem showed the right way to say, "Mary has a little lamb." The trick is making sure the subject and predicate agree! Now try your hand at some other Mother Goose rhymes. Write an *A* on the line if the subject and predicate agree. Write an *X* on the line if the subject and predicate do not agree.

_____ 1. Little Bo-Peep have lost her sheep.

_____ 2. Georgie Porgy, pudding and pie, kissed the girls and made them cry.

_____ 3. Three blind mice! See how they runs!

_____ 4. This are the house that Jack built.

_____ 5. Little Miss Muffet sat on a tuffet.

_____ 6. Some likes it hot; some likes it cold.

_____ 7. Humpty Dumpty sat on a wall.

_____ 8. Old King Cole were a merry old soul.

_____ 9. Jack and Jill went up the hill to fetch a pail of water.

_____ 10. When the wind blows, the cradle will rock.

_____ 11. Old Mother Hubbard went to the cupboard to give her poor dog a bone.

_____ 12. Little Tom Tucker sing for his supper.

25 Great Grammar Poems Scholastic Professional Books

The Gang of Three (Punctuation)

BACKGROUND

These three punctuation marks are sometimes called "sentence enders." A period ends a declarative sentence (*Mary slept soundly.*), follows most initials and abbreviations, and follows numerals when writing lists. Periods are also used in Web site addresses. A question mark ends an interrogative sentence (*Did you see that car?*). An exclamation point ends an exclamatory sentence (*I love it!*) or a strong imperative sentence (*Go away!*). An exclamation point also sometimes separates an interjection from a complete sentence (*Hooray! It's my birthday!*).

VOCABULARY

sparingly: ADVERB rarely; only when needed

dramatic: ADJECTIVE very noticeable

emphatic: ADJECTIVE giving importance to something

TEACHING THE POEM

Compare/Contrast
Invite students to read aloud examples of sentences with periods, exclamation points, and question marks from the poem. Ask students to listen carefully and compare how each type of sentence sounds. (Point out that a reader's voice rises toward the end of a question. A reader's voice sounds more urgent or excited when reading an exclamation than when reading a declarative sentence.)

Discussion
Ask students to think about why we don't use exclamation points on all our sentences (after all, don't we want all of our writing to be exciting?). For fun, rewrite a paragraph from a book or periodical you use in class, using all exclamation points. Distribute to students and invite them to read the paragraph aloud. Students will discover that when all sentences are read with the same urgency, none of the sentences stand out.

Creative Writing
Have students write a short story based on a recent class trip or school event. Urge students to use at least one period, one exclamation point, and one question mark in their stories.

Multicultural Studies
Invite bilingual students to share how sentences are punctuated in other languages. For example, in Spanish, a question has two question marks: one (upside down) at the beginning of the sentence and another (right side up) at the end.

Practice
Students can use the *Gang of Three* reproducible activity to practice selecting punctuation for different types of sentences (page 55).

Answers to Reproducible: 1. period **2.** exclamation point **3.** exclamation point **4.** question mark **5.** period **6.** question mark **7.** exclamation point **8.** period **9.** question mark **10.** period

The Gang of Three

At the end of a sentence, what do you see?
It's always one of the gang of three.

The Period

The period is just a dot,
but it gets to do a lot.
A period is at the end
each time you make a statement, friend.

The Question Mark

When does a question mark appear?
When do you ask a question, dear?
What do question marks all show?
There's something someone wants to know.

The Exclamation Point

(Use sparingly to be dramatic.)
Let's go, grammar!
Be emphatic!
Pitch that ball! Batter, bat it!
Hey, that play's a real sensation!
It deserves an exclamation!

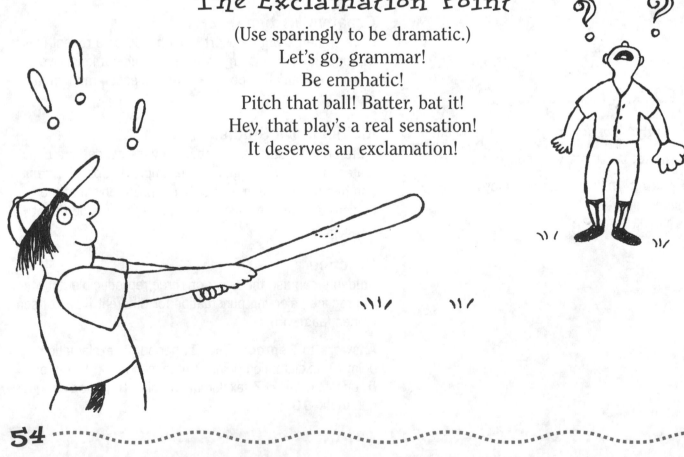

25 Great Grammar Poems   Scholastic Professional Books   © Bobbi Katz

The Gang of Three

Use the three punctuation marks described in the poems (period, question mark, and exclamation point) to complete the sentences below. Write the correct punctuation mark after each sentence.

1. Francine opened the refrigerator

2. Run for your life

3. Leave me alone

4. Do you know the way to the theater

5. Jenny's birthday is in October

6. May I borrow your pen

7. I am so excited

8. Bryan is going to get his hair cut

9. Are wolves related to dogs

10. Joseph went to the parade

11. Write a sentence that ends with a period.

_____

12. Write a sentence that ends with a question mark.

_____

13. Write a sentence that ends with an exclamation point.

_____

The Run-On Sentence

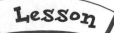

BACKGROUND

A run-on sentence is a sentence that should be broken into two or more sentences. It contains several separate thoughts and has more than one subject and predicate.

- Look at the time I am afraid I will miss my bus and then I will be late for soccer.

- Peter is very kind and thoughtful and we all love having him for a friend but he is moving to a different state soon so then we will miss him.

A corollary to the run-on sentence is the sentence fragment. A fragment does not contain the necessary subject and predicate and thus is not a complete sentence.

- When you get home.

- There, on the dining room table.

VOCABULARY

noodle-head: NOUN silly person

dissatisfaction: NOUN unhappiness

update: NOUN the latest information

TEACHING THE POEM

Discussion

This poem compares parts of speech—such as nouns and prepositions—to basketball players. Find a clue in the poem that tells how the "players" feel. *(They are puzzled, left dangling.)* Why are the players confused? *(Possible answer: The sentence is not stopping.)*

Discussion

Why are run-on sentences not a good idea? *(They confuse the reader.)*

Writing

Ask students to perform "sentence surgery" on the poem, rewriting the poem in complete sentences. Students may need to add words here and there to separate the sentences.

Practice

This poem is based on the concept of a sports report. Have students use the sports report on *The Run-On Sentence* reproducible activity (page 58) to break a run-on sentence into several smaller sentences.

Answers to Reproducible: Answers will vary.

The Run-On Sentence

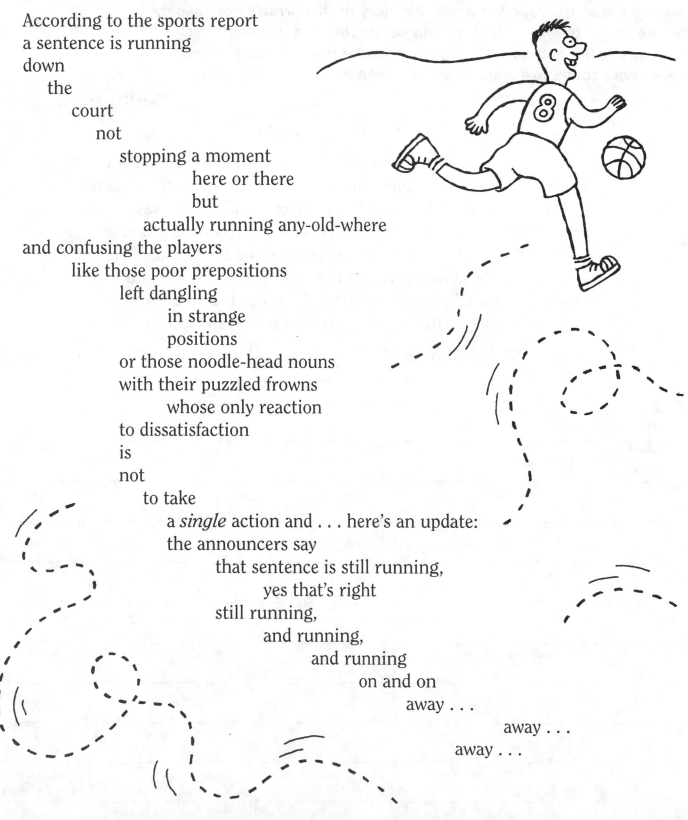

According to the sports report
a sentence is running
down
    the
        court
          not
            stopping a moment
                here or there
                but
            actually running any-old-where
and confusing the players
        like those poor prepositions
          left dangling
            in strange
            positions
       or those noodle-head nouns
       with their puzzled frowns
          whose only reaction
       to dissatisfaction
       is
       not
          to take
            a *single* action and . . . here's an update:
            the announcers say
                that sentence is still running,
                  yes that's right
              still running,
                and running,
                  and running
                    on and on
                      away . . .
                          away . . .
                    away . . .

25 Great Grammar Poems   Scholastic Professional Books   © Bobbi Katz

The Run-On Sentence

Harvey the sports reporter wrote this story for tomorrow's newspaper, but he forgot to break his story into sentences. Can you help? Use the lines at the bottom of the page to rewrite Harvey's story. If you need more room, use another sheet of paper.

A Big Win

The Tigers took first place in the county Little League last weekend with a win against the Bears the score of the final game of the season was 7 to 6 and Tiger player Tom Hughes was responsible for the winning run of course everyone is proud of Tom and the rest of the team and coach Celia Smart said, "These kids worked hard for every run they scored this season, and they deserve this win" she also said the Tigers celebrated their big victory with a trip to the Dairy Mart for ice cream sundaes.

_____

_____

_____

_____

_____

_____

_____

_____

_____

_____

25 Great Grammar Poems   Scholastic Professional Books

The Comma

BACKGROUND

Commas slow us down as we read, so, paradoxically, we comprehend more quickly. Commas help to separate ideas.

- They separate clauses in a sentence. (*The students cheered, which made the teacher smile.*)

- They separate items in a series. (*I need to buy some cereal, bread, and apples.*)

- They separate a city from a state. (*Philadelphia, Pennsylvania*)

- They separate a direct quotation from the speaker. (*He said, "Let's go."*)

- They separate the month and day from the year when writing the date. (*January 3, 1999*)

- They set apart appositives—descriptive phrases that modify a noun. (*Claudia, the class president, will speak.*)

VOCABULARY

deftly: ADVERB skillfully and quickly

drama: NOUN excitement or feeling

TEACHING THE POEM

Scavenger Hunt

List some of the comma functions described at left on the board. Invite students to work in small groups to locate an example of each function in printed material. Students can use newspapers, magazines, textbooks, posters, food containers, and so on. Award a small prize to the first group to find a comma in each category.

Writing

Have students create a large comma-shaped poster on oak tag. Students should fill the poster with rules for using commas and examples. Display the poster as a ready reminder for student writers.

Practice

Have students use the *Comma* reproducible activity to practice comma placement (page 61).

Answers to Reproducible:

1. Malibu, California
2. markers, paste
3. school, please
4. cats, birds, and fish
5. August 15, 1990
6. out, "The
7. wallpaper, and paint
8. Bakers, the Burnses
9. Paris, France
10. math, which
11. said, "I
12. Monday, September 3
13. hat, but
14. muffin, banana
15. go," Dad

The Comma

To separate,
    to pause,
        to wait,
            to add a bit of drama,
there's nothing that can do these things
more deftly than a comma.

25 Great Grammar Poems   Scholastic Professional Books   © Bobbi Katz

The Comma

There is a comma missing in each of the sentences below. Show your skills as a grammar detective! Draw a comma in the correct spot in each sentence.

1. I live in Malibu California.

2. We'll need markers paste, cardboard, and scissors to complete the project.

3. If you have time after school please clean your room.

4. Dogs, cats birds and fish are all popular pets.

5. Nora was born on August 15 1990.

6. Michael called out "The pizza is here!"

7. This store sells furniture, wallpaper and paint.

8. The Bakers the Burnses, and the DeLeons all live on Cedar Avenue.

9. Have you ever visited Paris France?

10. I got an A in math which made my parents happy.

11. The mail carrier said "I have a package for you."

12. On Monday September 3, the new school year will begin.

13. Tricia remembered her hat but she forgot her gloves.

14. I had a muffin banana, and juice for breakfast.

15. "It's time to go" Dad said.

Apostrophe

BACKGROUND

As the poem suggests, an apostrophe looks very much like a "high hook." It is used to show possession (*Sheila's sandal, the boys' books*) or to form contractions (*can't, she's, let's*). An additional use of the apostrophe not mentioned in the poem is to create plurals of letters and numerals (*I got all B's; My parents are in their 40's*).

VOCABULARY

versatility: NOUN usefulness in many ways

contraction: NOUN two words combined with an apostrophe

TEACHING THE POEM

Discussion
In the poem, the apostrophe describes itself as a "High Hook." Do you think that is a good description? Explain.

Writing
Brainstorm a list of contractions with students. Then, to help students remember that a contraction is two words put together, write a class adventure story explaining how contractions came to be. You might start with this prompt: "Did you know that the word *can't* used to be *can not*, and that *let's* was once *let us*? These words lost some of their letters many years ago—all thanks to a character known as High Hook. . . ."

Practice
It is common for students to leave out apostrophes in their own writing, even when they understand the apostrophe's functions. Have students practice writing words with apostrophes. You may also want to have kids find the apostrophe on the computer keyboard and practice typing this punctuation mark.

Practice
Students can explore apostrophes at greater length with the reproducible activity on page 64.

Answers to Reproducible: Contractions: she'll, won't we'd, wouldn't, I'll, let's, can't, shouldn't. Possessives: Sal's, kids', Abe's, Tina's, poets', Ellen's.

Apostrophe

Think High Hook
when you look for me.
Then see my versatility.
Taking two words,
I'll make a subtraction,
and **you'll** have one word.
It's called a contraction.

I must confess
my strange obsession.
I join with "s" to show possession.
Now Nora can't claim **Peter's** poodles,
and Peter won't eat **Nora's** noodles.

Contract!
Possess!
Ah, yes, that's me!
I may look like a comma,
but **I'm** an apostrophe!

25 Great Grammar Poems   Scholastic Professional Books   © Bobbi Katz

Apostrophe

The poem mentions two ways to use an apostrophe: to form a contraction or to create a possessive. Look at the words in the box. Decide which words are contractions and which are possessives, then write the words in the correct columns.

she'll	Abe's	can't
won't	wouldn't	poets'
we'd	I'll	Ellen's
Sal's	let's	shouldn't
kids'	Tina's	

CONTRACTIONS

_____

_____

_____

_____

_____

POSSESSIVES

_____

_____

_____

_____

_____

Write one sentence using a contraction.

_____

Write one sentence using a possessive.

_____

25 Great Grammar Poems Scholastic Professional Books

Quotation Marks

BACKGROUND

Quotation marks appear before and after a direct quote (a person's exact words). These marks also set apart song and poem titles, titles of articles in magazines and newspapers, and chapter titles in books. You may want to point out to students that single quotation marks are used to set off a quotation within a quotation.

VOCABULARY

fence: VERB to surround or mark off an area

TEACHING THE POEM

Drama
Have small groups of students dramatize the poem for the class. Encourage readers to dress in costume!

Discussion
Review with students the difference between summarizing a person's words (*He said he would meet us outside school*) and using a person's exact words (*He said, "I'll meet you just outside the school"*). Offer several examples and invite students to identify each statement as a summary or direct quote.

Writing
Newspaper articles are full of direct quotes. Have students read several news articles, then write their own articles using several quotations. Provide topics for students to choose from (for example, how the cafeteria staff plans a week's menu or what toys were popular when students' parents were young). Help students select a person to interview and quote.

Language Arts
When reading novels or picture books aloud in class, use different voices for different characters, or invite a different student to read each character's dialogue. This will heighten students' awareness of quotes.

Practice
Students can use the reproducible activity to review the correct placement of quotation marks (page 67).

Answers to Reproducible: 1. A **2.** B **3.** A **4.** C **5.** A **6.** B **7.** C

Quotation Marks

Who tells who says what?
We do!
We're on the job
in pairs
of two.
Quotations can't find

We fence them in

We fence them in
on either side.
"We fence them in!"
we said.

We do!
We're on the job
in pairs
of two.

a place to hide.

on either side.

We fence them in
on either side.
"We fence them in!"
we said.

Note: This poem should be read aloud by two people or two groups like a duet. One person reads the left side; another the right side. Both people read together when the same words are on the same line.

25 Great Grammar Poems   Scholastic Professional Books   © Bobbi Katz

Quotation Marks

Below are several examples of quotations. Find the quotation in each set that is punctuated properly. Circle the letter next to the quotation.

1. **A.** Colin shouted, "Run to third base!"
   B. Colin shouted, 'Run to third base!'
   C. Colin shouted Run to third base!

2. **A.** "Thanks for dinner, said Phoebe."
   B. "Thanks for dinner," said Phoebe.
   C. Thanks for dinner" said Phoebe.

3. **A.** My mom whispered, "It's a surprise."
   B. "My mom whispered," It's a surprise.
   C. My mom "whispered, It's a surprise."

4. **A.** Are you ready to order? asked the waiter.
   B. "Are you ready to order" asked the waiter.
   C. "Are you ready to order?" asked the waiter.

5. **A.** "I have big plans for this city," said the mayor.
   B. 'I have big plans for this city' said the mayor.
   C. "I have big plans for this city said the mayor".

6. **A.** The teacher said, "Let's read the poem now"
   B. The teacher said, "Let's read the poem now."
   C. The teacher said, "Let's read the poem now.

7. **A.** Hello! said Joanna.
   B. "Hello! said Joanna.
   C. "Hello!" said Joanna.

The Double Negative Is a No-No

BACKGROUND

A double negative occurs when the speaker or writer chooses both a negative verb (*will not, shouldn't, or can't*) and a negative object of the verb (*no, nothing, none*). Explain to students that in this case, the two "no's" cancel each other out—and form a "yes." For example, if a speaker wants to indicate that he is out of milk, he could say, "I have no milk left," or "I do not have any milk left." However, that "I don't have no milk left" actually means the speaker has plenty of milk!

VOCABULARY

intend: VERB to mean to do something

negative: ADJECTIVE giving the answer no

voided: VERB made something not count

TEACHING THE POEM

Discussion

This poem points out that it is incorrect to use phrases such as "don't have no time" or "can't get nothing." Ask students to brainstorm why these phrases do not make sense.

Simon Says

Add a grammar twist to this classic game. Line up your students and tell them to carefully follow your directions. Point out that if you use a double negative, it is really a positive. Then give the students a variety of instructions and watch how they respond.

■ Simon says you may take no steps forward. (Students should not move.)

■ Simon says you can't take no step. (Students should take a step, because of the double negative.)

Practice

Have students rewrite the sentences on the reproducible activity to avoid the double negative (page 70).

Answers to Reproducible: Sentences will vary. Negatives are: **1.** doesn't, no **2.** can't, no **3.** didn't, none **4.** not, nothing **5.** isn't, no **6.** doesn't, no **7.** don't, nothing **8.** won't, none

The Double Negative Is a No-No

Nina isn't shooting straight.
Jane can't get past the starting gate.
Joe does not intend to go.
I asked him once, and he said, "No."

These sentences all clearly say,
"It isn't happening, José."
See "not."
　　　See "isn't."
　　　　　See "can't."
　　　　　　　See "no."
They're the negative signals that let you know.
　　　But . . .
use two of them in one sentence, kid,
and you'll be sorry that you did.
One will cancel the other out.
No one will know what you're talking about.

He **doesn't** have **none**.
Then he MUST have some.
She **don't** like **nothing**.
Then she MUST like something.

The double negative should be avoided,
or what you're saying will be voided.

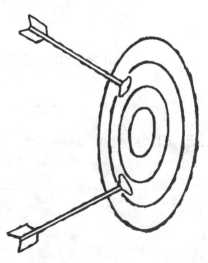

The Double Negative Is a No-No

**The sentences below all contain double negatives. Underline all the negatives.
Rewrite each sentence on the line to get rid of the double negative.**

1. Tim doesn't have no interest in sports.

_____

2. Mirtha can't drive no car until she is 16 years old.

_____

3. I shared my lunch with him because he didn't bring none.

_____

4. We should not do nothing until we hear the directions.

_____

5. Randy isn't no fool.

_____

6. That street doesn't have no houses on it.

_____

7. I don't know nothing about it.

_____

8. Chris won't listen to none of your stories.

_____

25 Great Grammar Poems Scholastic Professional Books

Notes

Notes